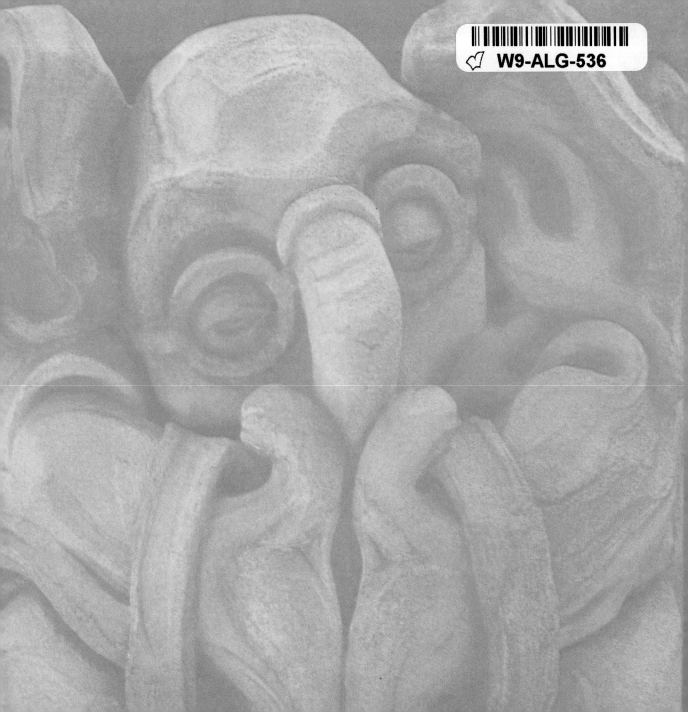

A M E R I C A N   G A R G O Y L E S

AMERICAN

GARGOYLES
SPIRITS IN STONE

DARLENE TREW CRIST

PHOTOGRAPHS BY ROBERT LLEWELLYN

CLARKSON POTTER/PUBLISHERS
NEW YORK

Published by Clarkson Potter/Publishers, New York, New York.
Member of the Crown Publishing Group.

Random House, Inc. New York, Toronto, London, Sydney, Auckland
www.randomhouse.com

CLARKSON N. POTTER is a trademark and POTTER and colophon are registered trademarks of Random House, Inc.

Printed in China

DESIGN BY JANE TREUHAFT

Library of Congress Cataloging-in-Publication Data
Crist, Darlene Trew.
   American gargoyles: spirits in stone / by Darlene Trew Crist; photographs by Robert Llewellyn—
1st ed. Includes bibliographical references and index.
   1. Gargoyles—United States—Themes, motives.   2. Decoration and ornament, Architectural—
United States.   I. Llewellyn, Robert.   II. Title.
NA3503.A1 C75 2001
729'.5—dc21   00-058475

ISBN 0-609-60685-9

10 9 8 7 6 5 4 3 2 1

First Edition

TO

Toy, Cyd,
and
Rishie

CONTENTS

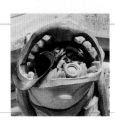

FOREWORD

This book, a primer on American gargoyles, is designed to inspire you to look up rather than down when walking along a city street. By changing your vantage point only slightly, odds are you will be surprised at the number of strange, fascinating, and generally weird-looking carved creatures that you've been missing.

Robert Llewellyn, a truly gifted photographer who has made these pages come alive, and I traveled across the United States looking up in search of gargoyles. Sound silly? It was—and great fun at that. We found many unique carvings and interesting buildings along the way. We took some circuitous routes through the bowels of major buildings, from Gothic cathedrals to cathedrals of commerce, such as the Woolworth Building in New York City, to get to their tops. Once we arrived at our destinations, we had the good fortune of seeing major metropolitan areas from heights that usually only ironworkers and roofers get to experience.

A brief overview of terms will be helpful before we share our journey into the world of American gargoyles. The traditional technical definition of a gargoyle is "a grotesquely carved figure of a human or animal with a spout that projects from a roof gutter and throws rainwater clear of the building"— in other words, a decorated downspout.

We have included here true gargoyles as well as gargoyle look-alikes, or, more accurately, grotesques. Grotesques don't

have water spouting from a mouth or other orifice; otherwise, they can hardly be distinguished from their carved cousins, gargoyles.

Regardless of its technical classification, each carving tells a unique story through its carved detail, its implied message, or how it came to be placed on a building. We provide as much information on the carvings as possible, but because of their very nature, detailed records were often not kept. In such cases, their stories are interpreted visually. Many of the carvings have been given names by the people who see them regularly, which we have used here. For others, we have taken the liberty of naming them ourselves, based on either a carving's appearance or what it represents.

We hope you will change your city strolling style after you read *American Gargoyles* and discover the many amazing carvings that seem to magically appear on buildings throughout the United States. Let this book serve as your guide. The sites we explore in these pages offer gargoyles either of unique interest or in such abundance that an outing to see them will be well worth the time. We uncovered a menagerie of gargoyles from the following places:

❧ WASHINGTON NATIONAL CATHEDRAL—This breathtakingly beautiful cathedral in our nation's capital is the clear winner in terms of number of gargoyles on one building—a total of 112.

❀ UNIVERSITY OF CHICAGO—
We could show only a sampling
of the hundreds of unique carvings located throughout this
large and lovely urban campus.

❀ WOOLWORTH BUILDING—
A few surprises exist near the
top of the "Cathedral of Commerce" on Broadway in New
York City.

❀ GRACE CATHEDRAL—
Visitors to San Francisco
should take a mandatory trol-
ley ride to the top of fashionable Nob Hill to see the

carvings on this architectural
masterpiece.

❀ CATHEDRAL CHURCH OF
ST. JOHN THE DIVINE—
We included the Cathedral of
St. John the Divine in New
York City, even though it has
no true gargoyles, because it
has many masterfully carved
grotesques.

❀ UNIVERSITY OF PENNSYL-
VANIA—The quadrangle at
Penn in Philadelphia was
designed to replicate those of
old European universities, and

intricate carvings appear every
four feet on the buildings that
surround it.

❀ TRIBUNE TOWER—This
Gothic monolith in downtown
Chicago pays homage to the
power and financial strength of
the American press, while its
exterior decoration pokes fun
at the role of the press and the
society in which it functions.

❀ CALVARY UNITED
METHODIST AND FIRST
PRESBYTERIAN CHURCHES—
Visitors to Pittsburgh will be

pleased to see that successful American industrialists donated some of their money to decorating their churches in elaborate and delightful ways.

❦ PRINCETON UNIVERSITY— Rich architectural detail confronted us at every turn on Princeton's campus in New Jersey. In spite of our best efforts to stay focused on gargoyles, we threw in a few photographs and stories of grotesques, because they were too fabulous to be overlooked.

On a personal note, pulling together this book has been an enriching experience. It was an honor and privilege to have had the opportunity to talk with many of the sculptors and carvers who created the featured gargoyles. I learned from these artisans how they captured their creativity and turned it into magical stone creatures. Their talent and skill deserve far more recognition than they receive.

This book also could not have been completed without a generous sharing of informa-tion. I am beholden to many people across the country— archivists, building manag-ers, and gargoyle experts and aficionados—who so kindly shared their knowledge of and enthusiasm about gargoyles with me. It was a great pleasure to be in the company of so many who share my appreciation for what, in reality, are merely deco-rated downspouts. To a one, they are gentle souls with a sense of humor.

1

SPIRITS IN STONE

PRIMITIVE ART FORM. SYMBOLIC ornamentation. Fancy downspouts. Gargoyles are all of these and more. ❊ First used in medieval Europe to lure pagans into Christian churches, gargoyles eventually made their way across the Atlantic Ocean as immigrant stone carvers brought their talents with them to the New World. Today, gargoyles can be found on a wide variety of American buildings—from stately neo-Gothic cathedrals to ivy-covered university dormitories to towering skyscrapers—as well as in homes,

offices, and gardens, or on key chains, necklaces, and tattoos as good-luck charms. Our fascination with gargoyles is, in many ways, a curiosity. Gargoyles are drainpipes. Their technical function is to move rainwater away from a structure. That's not very exotic, but people still love gargoyles. They are fun to look at. They make us wonder how and why they were placed on a particular building. And, they make us ponder their meaning.

To understand our present-day fascination with this ancient art form, it helps to look at the evolution of gargoyles. Decorative waterspouts have a fine and long tradition in the building arts. Some of the earliest examples were found within the volcanic remains of the city of Pompeii (A.D. 79), where lion's heads and animal shapes were used to conceal waterspouts. Both the Greeks and the Romans used animal-shaped stones as decorative waterspouts. Those primitive versions were the precursors to the "true" or carved gargoyles that date from the early twelfth century.

RIDGEBACK DRAGON (PREVIOUS PAGE)

Like the terrifying creatures that stand guard over Christian cathedrals, this menacing dragonlike creature stands guard over the Woolworth Building in New York City. Dubbed the "Cathedral of Commerce" shortly after its opening in 1913, the Woolworth Building is testimony to the earthly power of money and vision. Frank W. Woolworth, a farmer whose merchandising concept of five-and-ten-cent stores made him a household name and a fortune, wanted a building for his corporate offices that would tower above all others and be as impressive as any in the world.

The word *gargoyle* is derived from the French *gargouille,* whose Latin root, *gargula,* means gullet or throat. *Gargouille* is also connected to the French verb *gargariser,* "to gargle," which offers a more colorful description of the gargoyle's real mission.

Two colorful legends explain how gargoyles ended up on churches. The first involves La Gargouille, a dragon who was said to have regularly terrorized the French town of Rouen. On its annual visits, the dragon demanded of the townspeople a virgin maiden, although more often than not, he was given a convicted criminal instead. As the story goes, the villagers grew tired of La Gargouille's demands. A priest arrived upon the scene and promised to subdue the dragon if, in return, the townspeople would build and join his church. Doubting his chances for success, they readily agreed and the priest set off to confront the dragon.

Shortly after leaving town, the priest came upon La Gargouille. Using the sign of the cross and other Christian powers, he quickly subdued the beast, then led the docile dragon on a leash back to Rouen. Wanting to ensure their permanent freedom from their oppressor, the townspeople burned La Gargouille at the stake. The beast's head and neck did not burn, however, undoubtedly due to its lifelong habit of breathing fire, which had toughened its skin. The townspeople mounted these charred remains on their newly constructed church as a symbol of victory over evil. This story was set in stone when a dragon was carved on the exterior of the cathedral at Rouen, where it can be seen to this day.

The Celts are the source of a second legend. Renowned hunters, the Celts believed that the heads of their prey served a dual purpose—attracting luck and repelling evil. To take advantage of these magical powers, the Celts mounted the heads on sticks and placed them in a circle around their homes. This practice was later expanded to include hanging such "dead heads" directly on buildings in their settlements.

Early Christians in search of converts placed gargoyles on churches to entice pagans—their much-needed future parishioners—inside. It was thought that by replicating the pagan use of fearsome carvings without officially condoning it, churches would seem more inviting. The marketing power of this ploy was enhanced by the fact that most people could not read, so images and symbols had even greater impact than they do today. It was a strategy that worked. Churches grew in number and influence as the pagan belief system and many of its images were absorbed into Christianity.

Regardless of how gargoyles evolved, the practice of placing "dead heads" on buildings made its way through the ages and across the Atlantic Ocean. They have been created using the same tools and virtually the same techniques since their arrival upon these shores. Most of the time, a sculptor conceives an image and makes a model of it, which is then used by a skilled carver to carve the piece in stone. In rare instances, a stone carver may be given the go-ahead to create a piece from his imagination directly on the stone.

The relationship between sculptor and carver can be likened to that of a composer and musician. The result of their collaboration, whether wicked or holy in nature, is richly represented on select cathedrals, churches, and buildings in America.

FALLEN ANGEL

The idea of a church "for national purposes" was included in Pierre L'Enfant's plans for the Federal City as early as 1791, but it took Congress more than one hundred years to grant a charter to realize this vision. Designed by George Bodley, Henry Vaughan, Philip Hubert Frohman, and others as a "House of Prayer for all People," the foundation stone for the Cathedral Church of St. Peter and St. Paul was laid in 1907.

One hundred and twelve gargoyles, no two exactly alike, grace the exterior of Washington National Cathedral. In the 1980s, sculptor Jay Hall Carpenter designed eleven of the last gargoyles, including eight of its largest. One is this angel, who perilously clings to a tree, holding the two halos for which he was ejected from heaven for stealing. The carving, done in 1987 by Matthew Girard and Kurt H. Kiefer, suggests that earthly evils can emerge even in the afterlife: this angel pays the price for his sins by being caught forever between heaven and earth.

UPSIDE-DOWN HUMANOID

Washington National Cathedral receives no public funding of any kind and was built entirely with private contributions. One method of encouraging donations was to link them with specific features of the building as it was constructed. This gargoyle was donated in memory of Frederick Lear Fryer, a partner of architect Avery Faulkner, who was a member of the Cathedral Building Committee. This sculpture was designed by Tylden W. Streett, one of twelve winning contestants in the cathedral's 1959–60 Gargoyle Design Contest. Reportedly Streett sculpted the naked humanoid creature upside down so it could be seen by more than "God and birds." John Guarente carved the piece, which was installed in 1975.

17

GRIFFINS OF WASHINGTON NATIONAL CATHEDRAL

Griffins, fantastical creatures that are half eagle and half lion, have graced Gothic cathedrals for centuries. They were placed on churches to ward off evil and prevent dark forces from entering sacred spaces of worship. This tradition was carried on at Washington National Cathedral, which was built in the decorated Gothic style of architecture. Flying buttresses and the sheer force of gravity support its 150,000 tons of hand-carved stone and magnificent stained glass. Included as part of the cathedral's collection of carvings is a spectacular array of griffins, which demonstrate the amazing individuality of artistic expression in the creation of gargoyles.

DRAGON GRIFFIN

When funds were available, work proceeded at a rapid pace at Washington National Cathedral and record keeping often took second place to actual construction efforts. As a result, the sculptor, carver, and date of particular pieces are sometimes not known, which is the case for this griffin. All that is known about its creators is seen in its design and execution. The gargoyle depicts an intricately carved dragonlike creature with wings, ears, horns, and, interestingly, a comb on its nose.

BISHOP'S GARDEN GRIFFIN

The sculptor of this dragonlike creature with wings, ears, scales, fangs, and claws was also not recorded. John Guarente carved the piece, and it reflects the precise style and clear detailing that are characteristic of his technique. This is a fine representation of a classical griffin.

HORNED GRIFFIN

Carver John Guarente clearly had a knack for griffins. This magnificent winged creature has fangs, the paws of a lion, and a small horn atop its head. The sculptor for this piece was not recorded.

ATTACK GRIFFIN

This is another example of carver John Guarente's fine craftsmanship. Dragonlike features were added to a winged creature with the head of a lioness. Its scaled reptilian claws and small wings distinguish it from other griffins. The sculptor of the piece was not recorded, but according to other sculptors interviewed at the cathedral, Guarente's talent as a carver meant that he played an important role in the quality of the finished piece.

HORNED DEVIL

For a cathedral of its size and complexity, Washington National Cathedral was built at a frenzied pace. Many medieval cathedrals took twice as long to complete. From the time the foundation stone was laid in 1907 until the final stone was set atop the southwest tower eighty-three years later, an amazing amount of human effort, time, and talent was required. Private donations were an important part of the equation, making continued construction possible.

Donors were often sought to support the creation of the cathedral's stonework and sculptures; this devilish carving, installed in 1975, was made possible by funds donated by Helen and Leland Gardner. Constantine Seferlis, who designed and carved the piece, incorporated their surname into his design by adding a richly adorned basket of fruits and vegetables on the underbelly of the sculpture for all to see. The gentle image of the basket is in direct contrast to the evil devil: depicted as a human with a single horn at the top of his head, he carries a pitchfork.

EVIL NOT LISTENING

Rosemary Lee was a young woman when she submitted a winning design to the Washington National Cathedral's 1959–60 Gargoyle Design Contest. Her design was ultimately used to create two gargoyles on the cathedral, one larger than the other. Carved by John Guarente, this half-human figure with fingers stuck in its ears is said to represent "evil refusing to listen to the Word of God."

REFUSING THE
WORD OF GOD

Not wanting to listen—to the Word of God or otherwise—is a commonly depicted subject on Washington National Cathedral. Here are three variations on the theme: left, a lionlike creature uses its human hands to block the Word of God. Above right, a large creature that looks like a winged dog with oversize feet and eyes appears to be refusing to look at the consequences of its evil ways. The third gargoyle may have heard the Word of God but responded inappropriately. This naughty pelican look-alike, with hat and wings, is depicted with a mocking smirk that represents its refusal to hear the Word of God.

DEVILISH CHARACTER

Dedicated on Palm Sunday in 1905, the present First Presbyterian Church on Sixth Avenue in Pittsburgh is actually the congregation's fourth building to stand on the site. The heirs of William Penn, founder of the colony of Pennsylvania, donated 2.5 plots of land to the congregation in 1787. As the congregation grew in number, ever-larger buildings were constructed on the site, which is now literally in the center of downtown Pittsburgh.

Thirteen gargoyles dot the facade of its cathedral-like English Gothic front. Shown here is a devilish-looking gargoyle that protrudes from above an intricately carved turret.

SMILING LEOPARD AND JESUS

The Cathedral of St. John the Divine in upper Manhattan was constructed in three different phases over a 120-year period and remains unfinished today. Financial shortfalls, a lack of skilled craftsmen, two world wars, and changes in leadership and priorities have all contributed to this slow-going process. Howard Quirk, a tour guide and author of the latest history of the cathedral, explains, "Its incompleteness matches that of humankind."

The cathedral is a rich combination of Romanesque, Byzantine, and Gothic architectural styles. In 1892, a design by the New York architectural firm Heins & LaFarge was selected from a field of one hundred, and the cornerstone was laid. An initial phase of Romanesque style makes up the easternmost portion of this grandiose cathedral, which at 601 feet is the longest in the world.

Noted sculptor Gutzon Borglum was awarded the contract to sculpt more than seventy-five pieces that grace the interior and exterior of the elaborate structure, including the one pictured here. His carvings are a remarkable evocation of different moods. The creature on the left has a protective posture, while the one on the right projects peace and benevolence as they both stand watch over young Jesus.

ANGEL BY ANGEL

John Angel (1881–1960) was an artist of some renown when he was awarded the contract to sculpt the west facade of the Cathedral of St. John the Divine in New York City. For the next twenty-two years, from 1925 to 1947, he presided over the intricate carving of literally thousands of pieces, including the angel pictured here.

Born and educated in England, Angel came to the United States at the invitation of Ralph Adams Cram of Cram and Ferguson, the architectural firm that altered the look of the cathedral to a more Gothic style. Angel's work at the cathedral brought him commissions from all over the country. His sculptures can be found at St. Patrick's Cathedral in New York City; the National Shrine of the Immaculate Conception in Washington, D.C.; the Presbyterian Church in East Liberty, Pennsylvania; St. Paul's School in Concord, New Hampshire; and the Cathedral of St. Paul in St. Paul, Minnesota.

REPTILIAN WITH WINGS

Niches on the Cathedral of St. John the Divine in New York City are filled with myriad saints, martyrs, and modern-day heroes. Pictured here on the Romanesque portion of the cathedral is a masterfully executed carving of a bird with the intertwined features of a reptile and dog, standing guard over the statue of Joseph in the niche below. Sculptor Gutzon Borglum created these pieces.

Borglum's contract for seventy-five pieces was huge, and the task was compounded by his perfectionist nature, great talent, and, some say, feisty temperament. At one point, he threatened to discontinue his work unless something was done to improve the carving. In a letter to architects Heins & LaFarge on January 24, 1907, he wrote: "The work is assuming such proportions, and the character of it is deteriorating rather than improving, that some radical change in methods of reproducing my work must be adopted if the work is to continue."

Borglum was given the control he sought. Much of the work he thought unacceptable was redone, and a shop was set up on the cathedral grounds so he could more easily supervise the execution of his work.

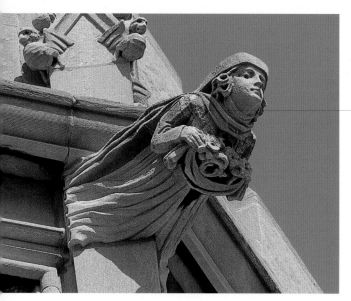 

GOD'S CREATURE

Atop a campus building that originally housed the geology and geography departments at the University of Chicago, and surrounded by birds and beasts, the angel shown above left brings a sense of spirituality to an otherwise decidedly secular building with a secular mission. One can only assume that its creator believed there was more to life than the subject of earthly studies. This carving is found on Rosenwald Hall, which was designed by the architects William Holabird and Martin Roche and erected in 1915.

THE DEVIL

Henry Ives Cobb designed the University of Chicago and his influence is still felt there today. He laid out a campus plan based on six quadrangles grouped around a seventh, which provided for a unified theme. He developed a collegiate Gothic architectural style to replicate the ambience of such highly respected European universities as Oxford and Cambridge. Different architects were selected to design individual campus buildings, which provided variation in style. Visual interest was further enhanced by a plethora of intricate carvings on the exteriors. One such devilish character is pictured above right.

MOSES AND THE
TEN COMMANDMENTS

A lion representing Moses holds the Ten Commandments atop the Leon Mandel Assembly Hall at the University of Chicago. Below Moses lies an intricate carving guaranteed to keep evil seekers away from the prophet and his message.

Named after its donor, a Chicago merchant, Mandel Hall has played an important role in the cultural life of the University of Chicago. Its thousand-seat theater has been the site of many performances, including the Chicago Symphony Orchestra, which first played there in 1904. A renovation was undertaken in 1981 that restored the facility to its original beauty and enhanced the acoustics and sight lines, making the interior as interesting as the exterior.

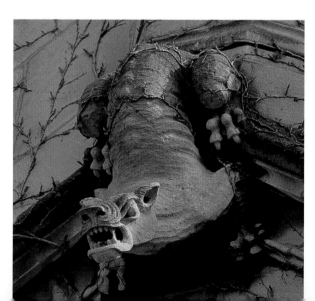

BATS IN THE BELFRY

Tribune Tower on Michigan Avenue in downtown Chicago is a stunning Gothic celebration of the American press. To mark its seventy-fifth anniversary in 1922, the *Chicago Tribune* newspaper launched an international design competition to build "the most beautiful and distinctive office building in the world." The design of architects John Mead Howells and Raymond M. Hood was selected from a field of 263 entries in competition for a $50,000 award.

Howells and Hood combined the efficiencies of a modern skyscraper with the beautiful lines and ornamentation of Gothic structures. One of the striking aspects of their design is the decorated tower at the top of the thirty-six-story structure. The tower with its arches and spires, and its sculpted carvings of bats in the belfry, is evocative of the medieval churches that inspired the design.

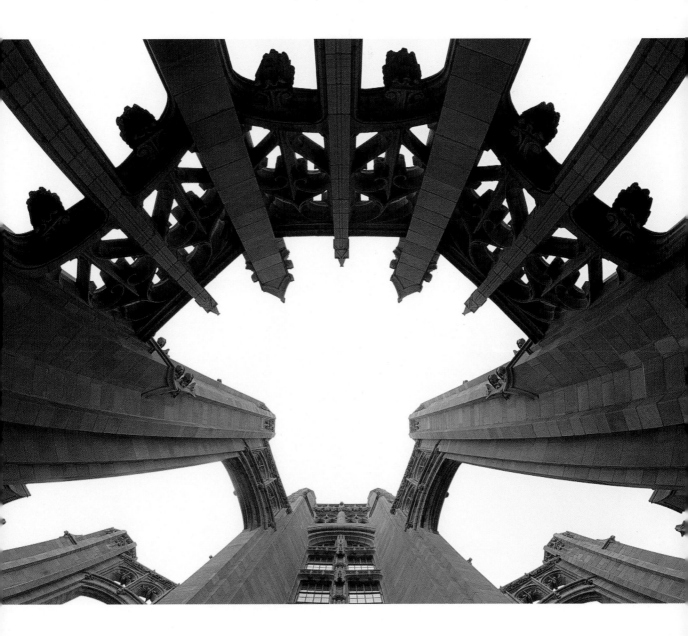

2

NOT QUITE GARGOYLES

GROTESQUES ARE OFTEN CONFUSED with gargoyles because of their similarity in material and subject matter. Only a true gargoyle aficionado ever pays much attention to the differences that separate one from the other, for they are more a matter of function than of form. ❧ Simply put, a gargoyle is a decorated downspout that directs water away from its building through a drainpipe in its mouth or another orifice. Grotesques lack the internal pipe of gargoyles, but in some instances do serve a water-carrying function

37

by directing water over their heads, although this usually is more happenstance than part of an integrated plan to keep water away from a structure.

The key difference between a gargoyle and a grotesque is that a grotesque's primary function is decorative; thus, they are found in a greater variety of locations than are gargoyles. A grotesque is a carving of a weird or supernatural animal or a group of weird animals. But, like their gargoyle kissing cousins, modern grotesques are often carved in a friendlier, more lighthearted manner.

Other terms are used to describe this grotesque mix. The French distinguish between working gargoyles and purely decorative carvings, which they call *chimères*. If a *chimère* is a carving of something strange or supernatural, it is referred to as a grotesque. A boss, a raised area used as ornamentation, is also considered a grotesque when carved in a weird or surreal shape.

Today, the generic term used to describe all of these decorative features is *gargoyle*. Few viewers

TURRET OF TERRIBLES (PREVIOUS PAGE)

A menagerie of beastlike creatures festoons a turret on the Cathedral of St. John the Divine in upper Manhattan. The grotesque carvings appear to stand guard over the sanctified grounds in the company of the archangel Gabriel. Sculptor Gutzon Borglum apprenticed at St. John and went on to sculpt for Princeton University (see page 85). He later gained national prominence for sculpting the presidential heads on Mount Rushmore in South Dakota. Borglum designed his carvings in a three-part process. First, the carving was modeled in clay. Next, a mold was made and filled with plaster of Paris. After the material hardened, the mold was chipped away to reveal an exact replica of the clay model. Carvers used such replicas as visual guides during the final step of carving in stone.

take the time to make the distinction, not only because of a general lack of architectural knowledge, but also because each decorative feature shares common attributes. Gargoyles and their counterparts serve to break up the lines of massive structures; they also add visual interest to exteriors and make them more engaging and aesthetically pleasing. Moreover, many modern carvings depict the activities carried on within the interior of a building and thus help define the structure by its purpose.

The majority of sculptures featured in this book were carved of limestone, most of which came from one quarry in Bloomington, Indiana; occasionally, other materials were used. For example, the grotesques on the Woolworth Building in New York were cast from terra cotta, a claylike material that is molded and fired. At Calvary United Methodist Church in Pittsburgh, builders took advantage of local materials and carved the grotesques from Cleveland bluestone. Lead-coated copper was used to create the carvings atop Grace Cathedral in San Francisco.

The materials used determine the longevity of the carvings. Acid rain, which causes pitting, rounding, and erosion of the sculptures, threatens those made of limestone. These effects are already visible on many of the gargoyles in the northeastern United States. Some are at greater risk than others, for the rate of decay depends on the specific composition of the stone used and its actual exposure to the elements. Thus, carvings that are more sheltered fare better than those on the unprotected edges of structures.

This chapter includes a variety of carvings that are not true gargoyles in order to illustrate how they are both different from and similar to the "real thing."

WYVERNS OF GRACE CATHEDRAL

At the top of San Francisco's fashionable Nob Hill neighborhood stands Grace Cathedral, its design inspired by the thirteenth-century French cathedrals of Notre Dame and Amiens. Eight identical grotesques encircle the lantern portion of the central spire, or fleche, which is 117 feet tall from the roof ridge, making it the tallest Gothic-style fleche in the western United States.

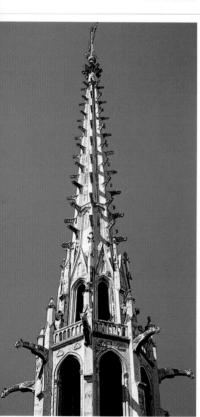

The grotesques represent wyverns (pronounced *wiverns*), two-legged winged dragons of medieval legend. Each is 4½ feet long and 1½ feet tall where it meets the main structure. They are depicted leaning forward on their talons with back-swept wings as though about to take flight. "One can think of wyverns as sort of 'holy pit bulls,' whose job is to dispel the evil forces, lightning, plague, war, and other calamities that may threaten the cathedral and city," explains Michael D. Lampen, archivist at Grace Cathedral. The protective power of such mythological creatures is a concept that predates Christianity; similar figures were found on the prows of Viking long ships.

Lewis Hobart was the original architect for the cathedral, although the architectural firm of Weihe, Frick and Kruse oversaw the completion of construction and worked diligently to ensure that the original design was followed. Construction on the cathedral began in 1927, but the fleche remained a stump until 1963, when a huge crane was used to lift the lantern and top shaft into position. It was at this time that the grotesques were fabricated from lead-coated copper by Fire Protection Products of San Francisco and added to the exterior.

PERFORMERS

FISHERBOY WITH HORN

A half boy–half fish nonchalantly blows a horn. Note the level of detail of this carving, from the well-defined biceps to the exaggerated eyebrows to the look of ease as the fisherboy blows notes into the wind.

GIRL WITH SQUIRREL

Pied piper or not? In her endeavor to make music, this grotesque has attracted the attention of an admiring squirrel.

DEVILISH CLOWN

Giving the appearance of being ready to leap off the building at any moment, this jester has the horns of a devil. Viewers are left to ponder which trait might dominate.

ATHLETES

FOOTBALL PLAYER

This receiver has caught the pass and shows no indication of relinquishing the ball! Note the exaggerated features, such as the ball's laces and the lines on the player's face that define activity and emotion.

DISCUS THROWER

This athlete appears to have jumped straight out of the original Olympic games. Complete with curls, flying cape, and discus, the grotesque seems ready to charge off to the next athletic challenge.

GLOBAL SOCCER PLAYER

Time and weather have taken a toll on the quadrangle carvings as evidenced by the state of this figure. The corrosive effects of acid rain prevent us from knowing for certain whether this scholar sits upon the globe pondering world events or if he is merely an aging soccer player contemplating the secrets of the game.

BALL HOMAGE

With biceps like these, this grotesque has got to represent an athlete. Observers are left guessing as to which sporting activity requires such undivided attention.

WEIRD MIXES

WOMAN WITH LIZARD

Here is an excellent example of the intertwining of human and animal features. Note the lizard's womanly face and hands mixed with a reptilian body.

GRIM REAPER

Life and death are companions in this gruesome twosome, below. A blind, hooded man fondly caresses a skeleton for all to see, serving as a reminder that death is only a breath away.

CHERUB WITH MAD MONKEY

Good and evil are portrayed in the above carving. The young cherub is about to lose its struggle with an imaginary beast that appears to be a combination of mad monkey and reptile.

SPLIT PERSONALITIES

HUMANOID BEAST

Half gorilla? Half man? Half ram? No written record exists regarding what this beastly carving may represent. It is presented here to illustrate the imaginative combination of human and animal features in a single carving.

TWO-HEADED JESTER

This grotesque is an example of two-headed carvings found at the corners of many of the quadrangle buildings. Here each head strains to keep a watchful eye on its territory.

VISIONARIES

COPE AND STEWARDSON

The architects poked fun at themselves in this carving, where they depicted their creative effort as that of a fool holding a basket of apples.

GOLD MAKER

A medieval alchemist is captured here in his attempt to change base metals into gold.

WISE WOMEN

YOUNG, OLD, AND IN-BETWEEN

Of special interest is the characterization of women on the buildings of a university that excluded them until the courts ordered their admission in 1877. Depicted here are three ages of the "opposite sex," from a young girl at above left to an older woman at right.

ST. JOHN THE DIVINE AND
THE FOUR HORSEMEN OF THE APOCALYPSE

A statue of the cathedral's namesake is prominently featured in the center of the main portal of the Cathedral of St. John the Divine in New York City. This magnificent depiction of the theologian was sculpted by John Angel, who later added a carving at the base of the pedestal that depicts the Four Horsemen of the Apocalypse, one of whom carries a bomb.

Like his predecessor, Gutzon Borglum, Angel had complaints about the quality of workmanship at the cathedral. In a letter to architects Cram and Ferguson dated May 13, 1947, Angel wrote, "The Unions will undoubtedly kill the carving profession." He went on to accuse union bosses of "stooping to any deceit or lie in order (as they think) to favour the interests of the carvers whom they dominate." Angel's complaints ultimately were answered when he, like Borglum some fifty years before him, was given greater control over the final carved pieces.

OPENMOUTHED EAGLE

The reality faced by the architects of the Woolworth Building was that in the early 1900s, it was simply impractical to build a Gothic skyscraper. Construction requirements such as regular steel support beams and frequent window openings limited the medieval quality of a structure that was to rise fifty-five stories into the air. Cass Gilbert, the building's architect, overcame these obstacles, however, and achieved a Gothic look on a modern skyscraper through extensive ornamentation and detailing on its exterior. This accomplishment was made possible by his use of terra cotta, a type of clay that hardens to stonelike strength yet is less costly and more flexible to work with than the stone it imitates. Almost the entire building is covered with terra-cotta ornamentation. Grotesques project from the twenty-sixth, forty-ninth, and fifty-first floors. Originally, thirty-five gargoyles protruded from the turrets, but because of deterioration only four remain; the others were removed during a major restoration of the structure that was launched in 1977 and completed in 1981. A dozen smaller carvings still grace what remains one of the grandest office buildings in the world.

MOTHER GOOSE

An unexpectedly gentle carving appears
on the biology wing of Princeton University's Guyot Hall. Its impassive expression brings to mind the Mother Goose of
fairy-tale fame. Laurel Masten Cantor,
director of creative services at Princeton
University, who has extensively studied
the gargoyles on campus, provides this
interpretation: "The carvers here were
really let loose to create whimsical
images. All over campus one can see how
they had fun with the students, professors, and academic endeavors taking
place. Perhaps, by depicting a character
from one of the stories from which we
learn how to read, this carving was an
attempt to show students' evolution.
After all, we begin with nursery rhymes
and ultimately go on to Shakespeare."

PANTHER

Ready to leap down from its high perch on Pittsburgh's Calvary United Methodist Church, this panther was carved by a Texan who purportedly wore a ten-gallon hat while he worked. Except for his headgear and his obvious talent, little else is known about the carver, including his name. General contractor George A. Cochrane hired Clark Brothers Stone Contractors of Allegheny, Pennsylvania, as stonecutters for the project. Although the Clark Brothers—John, James, and George—cut the stone, they apparently didn't have the skill needed to execute the carvings so they imported the unknown Texan to do the job. The carver worked from drawings provided by the architectural firm of Vrydagh and Shepard of Kansas City, working in association with Thomas B. Wolfe of Pittsburgh, which was hired in 1892 to design the church. Its twelve well-executed carved creatures that decorate the roof around its two mismatched spires are reminiscent of Chartres Cathedral in France.

The church's conglomeration of styles was allegedly influenced by Thomas B. Wolfe's trek through Europe. Architectural critic James D. Van Trump described Calvary Church as "a pastiche of medieval features." Constructed of Cleveland bluestone, the lovely edifice is a one-of-a-kind treasure that reflects the affluence of its original members. The building committee consisted of many Pittsburgh notables—including industrialist Charles C. Scaife, who made his fortune in steel, Durbin Horne and C. B. Shea of the successful Joseph Horne department store, and others. The committee instructed Vrydagh and Shepard to come up with a design that would reflect well upon their status, a goal that was accomplished with intricate detail and ornamentation, thirty-foot-high Tiffany windows, and a grandness of design that belies the building's actual role as a small neighborhood church.

MORE THAN ANIMALS

"I think the reason that the grotesques on the exterior of Tribune Tower are powerful is that they have some meaning and tell a story that reflects our culture. They also help bring this very tall building down to a human scale, making it perfectly sized to humans so that it feels innately comfortable," explains Blair Kamin, architecture critic for the *Chicago Tribune*.

Over the years, each of the grotesques that decorate Tribune Tower has come to represent a specific aspect of the city's culture, or a trait of its people, as a few select interpretations reveal.

WISE OLD OWL

Shown gripping a camera, the wise old owl on Tribune Tower illustrates observation and caution, qualities that are usually acquired with age.

IMPOVERISHED CAT

A cat that is forever captured in stone on Tribune Tower as a beggar with a tin cup in hand depicts the consequences of improvidence.

PROUD PORCUPINE

A porcupine with a horn in his paws appears neither open-minded nor humble, revealing the failings of intolerance and arrogance.

3

SACRED SCARECROWS

THE GARGOYLES OF YORE WERE menacing creatures often placed on churches and cathedrals to offer protection: they served as sacred scarecrows to ward off evil from the hallowed places below. They also could be viewed as reminders to the living of the consequences of sin, capturing condemned souls on their way to damnation and forever holding them prisoner in stone. But some gargoyles were benign figures who offered good fortune to all those who entered the churches.

Animal gargoyles were used to convey this entire range of references. Some represented specific spiritual conditions, both saintly and sinful. For example, serpents, foxes, and wolves were commonly used to depict the devil. Three of the four apostles had his own representative animal: Mark was depicted as a lion, Luke as an ox, John as an eagle, and only Matthew was depicted as a man. A dove represented the Holy Spirit and a lamb the son of God. A peacock was the symbol of eternal life.

Many American gargoyles also depict animals, but their spiritual connections are not as direct or as strong as those of their medieval counterparts, even where one might expect them to be. For example, a sculpture of a dog graces the main entrance of the Cathedral of St. John the Divine in New York City. The dog is not believed to represent either a sinner or a saint; a bishop's pet corgi was its model. Likewise, a donor's poodle was the inspiration for a carving on Washington National Cathedral.

FEMININE PIG (PREVIOUS PAGE)

The leadership of Washington National Cathedral was adept at maximizing its limited resources over the course of the more than eighty years construction. An example of how costs were kept to a minimum was a gargoyle design contest held in 1959–60. In spite of onerous submission requirements that included a finished model mounted on an armature, hundreds of would-be sculptors submitted their designs for a chance to live in perpetuity on our nation's cathedral. This winged creature with cloven hooves and sawtooth eyelashes was one of the designs selected. Completed in 1962, it was one of sculptor Constantine Seferlis's first carvings at the cathedral.

Location and the passage of time have lessened gargoyles' spiritual connection. Dragons, while still prominently featured on churches and other religious structures, no longer have the power to instill the fear of damnation. Likewise, the monkey carvings found throughout Princeton University's campus are there for no other reason than to symbolize the rambunctious behavior of the student population.

Both modern animal gargoyles and those of the past express human or humanlike characteristics, although time has altered interpretations. Gestures that today would be considered rude, crude, and even lewd were often integral parts of medieval carvings. The tongue, for example, was a regular and prominent feature of ancient gargoyles. More often than not, it was depicted as being "stuck out," which during the medieval period was believed to increase its protective power but today would have an insulting, lewd, or even playful meaning.

Greater sexual expressiveness also existed in earlier animal carvings. In the Middle Ages, gargoyles were frequently depicted pointing to their private parts or proudly displaying their genitalia. In pagan times, sexual organs symbolized fertility and early Christians displayed them on gargoyles as a means to embarrass congregations into chastity. Greater sexual explicitness could also be a result of the carvers' freedom to express themselves in pieces that would be placed near the tops of buildings, where few could see the finished products. Today, the lack of sexually explicit carvings may have more to do with the need for donor approval and corporate image making than social mores.

FRENCH POODLE

When given the assignment to carve a gargoyle in the shape of a dog for Washington National Cathedral, sculptor Jay Hall Carpenter decided on a French poodle because "the poodle's long nose is a good prominent feature. Along with its elegant body shape, the poodle lent itself to the fine detailing needed for a memorable gargoyle design."

The French poodle is one of only two gargoyles on the cathedral that lack a traditional mouth opening. (The other is the Crooked Politician; see page 96). Before carving was started, a gargoyle stone was usually drilled all the way through to accommodate the lead pipe used for drainage. But in this instance, the poodle was a replacement for a gargoyle that had been rejected after it was carved but before it was installed. A blank stone took its place on the building. Drilling a hole into a block of stone that had already been put in place would have been far too expensive an undertaking. As a solution, Carpenter designed this replacement with a slot running along the top of its head to provide for the necessary drainage. Walter Arnold carved this piece in situ in 1981.

FLOWER DOG

Modern gargoyles inevitably reveal the era in which they were created. A good example of this is Flower Dog at Washington National Cathedral. Its anonymous donor, a Washington art historian and dog lover, requested a happy, imaginative animal with curly hair and a flower. With this directive, artist Carl L. Bush designed a small, longhaired dog wearing flowers. Installed in 1969, this gargoyle is a charming reminder of the era's "flower children." Constantine Seferlis was the carver.

AFRICAN DOG

This gargoyle depicts a basenji, a small African dog renowned for its lack of a bark. The design was one of twelve selected from Washington National Cathedral's 1959–60 Gargoyle Design Contest. Artist Elizabeth Cannon Kimball based her drawing on her own basenji and is reported to have said, "Just think, a thousand years from now, we can look up and see my very own gargoyle!" To which her son supposedly replied, "I would rather think that a thousand years from now, we could look down and see it." Constantine Seferlis carved the piece, which was installed in 1964.

ROOSTER UNDER ATTACK

Situated on Washington National Cathedral, this rooster seems to be getting its life sucked out right before our eyes. Carver Constantine Seferlis explained that the snake represents evil attempting to destroy a living creature. Seferlis's precise attention to anatomical detail, evident here, gives his gargoyles both a clear identity and a defined message. Artist Peter Rockwell designed the piece in 1976.

AMERICAN RATTLESNAKE

"Because Washington National Cathedral is an American cathedral, my wife and I thought it deserved a truly American symbol. A 'Don't Tread on Me' snake seemed to be the perfect choice for our carving," explains Dr. Charles S. Tidball, who jointly designed this carving in 1966 with his wife, Dr. M. Elizabeth Tidball. Both Tidballs are retired medical school professors who taught at George Washington University; they have been active participants at Washington National Cathedral for years.

Dr. Charles Tidball recounts how he and his wife were encouraged to donate and design a gargoyle: "On a late fall evening when fog had all but hidden the Central Tower from view, former dean Francis B. Sayre pointed to it and asked if my wife and I had ever been to its top. Of course we hadn't, so the next day Dean Sayre took us on a tour. At the top, it was easy for him to convince us to make a permanent addition to the cathedral's carvings. Who could have refused?"

The Tidballs were given a block of clay one-quarter the size of an actual gargoyle and set to work. To evoke the fearsomeness of traditional gargoyles, they designed their snake in attack, with open mouth and visible fangs. Carver John Guarente added rattles to both sides of the piece so that it could be identified as an American rattler from either direction.

WILD BOAR

Washington National Cathedral was a massive undertaking. Unlike other projects of this kind, a concerted effort was made to document and catalog the design and construction. Nonetheless, the creators of this gargoyle in the shape of a wild boar were not recorded. The talents of sculptor and carver are much in evidence here in this lighthearted approach to a wild-and-woolly boar.

PERCHERON HORSE

The Percheron Horse with its corn stalk honors the rich farmlands of America. The donor hailed from the farming counties of Kane and De Kalb in Illinois. Appropriately, the gargoyle was placed on the side of the cathedral that overlooks the Bishop's Garden.

Installed in 1970, this gargoyle was sculpted by Carl L. Bush and carved by Frederick E. Hart under the tutelage of master carver Roger Morigi. Hart, a high-school dropout, became an excellent carver and a sculptor in his own right. He was one of the few craftsmen who worked at Washington National Cathedral to gain national recognition for his skill.

GOAT

This goatlike creature on Washington National Cathedral clearly demonstrates sculptor and carver Constantine Seferlis's appreciation of anatomy. He took an ordinary animal and exaggerated its features for dramatic effect. Seferlis's philosophy about good gargoyle design is that "you really don't have to fool around much with the perfection of anatomy to make a gargoyle that achieves its intent—that is, to scare someone or make them laugh . . . maybe even cry."

WEEPING SEA TURTLE

A weeping sea turtle and the sad-eyed seagull that shares its perch on Washington National Cathedral graphically depict the threatened state of our environment. Installed in 1976 in memory of an environmentalist who worked for the protection of giant turtles, this gargoyle makes a direct political statement in a heart-wrenching way. Sculpted and carved by Constantine Seferlis, the piece demonstrates how effectively stories can be told and messages relayed through this artistic medium.

71

RABBIT AND SNAKE

"Animals are good subjects for gargoyles because their realness gives people something to attach to," says classically trained sculptor Constantine Seferlis. Here, the rabbit and the snake appear frighteningly real on Washington National Cathedral. The rabbit's terror of his impending fate is clearly evident as he awaits the outcome of the contest between predator and prey.

STYLIZED EAGLE

"In other places at Washington National Cathedral, the creative process was pretty well controlled. But because gargoyles were on its exterior and often high enough up so they could only be seen by birds, they offered a wonderful opportunity for a sculptor to express himself," explains Jay Hall Carpenter, who began his career at Washington National Cathedral when he was seventeen as a stone carver's assistant.

Part of this freedom of expression is evident in the sculptors' interpretation of common themes. Here, Carl L. Bush presents his version of an eagle. His has a bit more style, panache, and levity than do others of its kind. The carver of the piece was not recorded.

RAM

Constantine Seferlis designed and carved this wonderful ram on Washington National Cathedral, and it stands as a fine example of artisanal talent. The sculpture depicts a ram with elongated horns, protruding eyes, low ears, and cloven hind feet.

COMPOSITES

Many gargoyles are not clearly identifiable as specific animals and are perhaps better understood as composite figures. Like their historical counterparts the griffin and the wyvern, these creatures combine parts of animals to form new ones. The result is an interesting and often amusing visual experience.

FISH

Sculpted and carved by Carl L. Bush, this gargoyle on Washington National Cathedral, above left, has a number of readily identifiable fish features—scales, fins, and flippers—along with a number of nonfish features, such as its two top knots and the drool running from the side of its mouth. The result is a carving that elicits disgust and even fear in younger viewers.

UNICORN

Looking ready to go to a children's birthday party with a horn atop its head, this wacky creature, right, was designed and carved by John Guarente, who gave it wings, lion paws, and big teeth to inspire fear in all.

MULE

Demonstrating a desire to showcase all possible variations on God's creatures, a mulelike beast, opposite, on Washington National Cathedral was given floppy ears, three horns atop its head, and incisors that only the foolish would mess with. The sculptor is not known, but Oswald Delfrate carved the piece.

VARIATIONS ON A THEME

First Presbyterian Church in Pittsburgh was designed by architect Theophilas Parsons Chandler in a modified English Gothic style. Arthur H. Williams' Sons of Philadelphia was hired on as contractor to oversee the construction of the elaborate building crafted from hard sandstone. The design called for fourteen gargoyles (thirteen of which still exist). The two eagle gargoyles here demonstrate how designers would often choose a common body structure and alter it slightly to make each carving unique. Ram horns were added to the eagle above to differentiate it from the eagle below, whose ears resemble those of a dog.

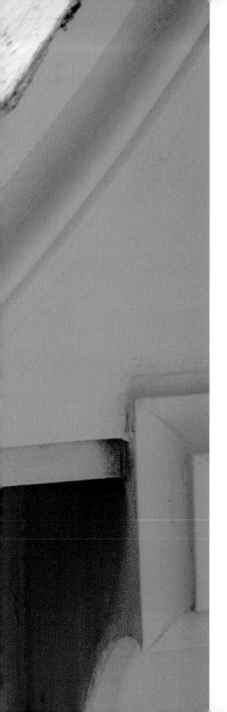

SMILING DRAGON

Frank Woolworth spared no expense in building the structure that would bear his name. He hired two men—architect Cass Gilbert and builder Louis J. Horowitz—then ultimately spent $13.5 million in cash to cover construction costs of the "world's tallest building," which stands at 792 feet from street level. [The only taller structure at the time (1913) was the Eiffel Tower in Paris, which stands at 895 feet.]

Cass Gilbert combined his love of ornate Gothic architecture with his knowledge of building construction requirements to design a remarkable building for its time. Louis J. Horowitz, president of the Thompson-Starrett Company, conquered the tremendous challenges posed in constructing the fifty-five-story elaborate Gothic structure, weight being one among many.

As part of the solution, the grotesques that decorate the Woolworth Building in New York City were made from terra cotta rather than stone. Baked at high temperatures to create a hard, durable ornamental tile, terra cotta can be used to create pieces that are hollow and thus lighter than those made of solid stone. The clay can be easily molded, and as a result it can be cast into any shape, and glazed to look like sculpted stone or enameled metal.

To achieve his desired effect, architect Gilbert hired John Donnelly and Eliseo Ricci to sculpt all of the designs for the building. Sculpting in terra cotta was a multi-step process. First, a model was created. If Gilbert approved it, a plaster mold was then made from the model and clay was pressed into it. After the clay began to stiffen, the mold was disassembled to expose the clay, which was allowed to air-dry further. A final finish or glaze was applied to the piece before it was fired.

FROG AND BAT

In the Middle Ages, frogs were considered a symbol of lewdness. Whether this interpretation applies to those that dot the twenty-sixth floor of the Woolworth Building in Manhattan is a subject of debate. There the frogs—lewd or not—are joined by bats, owls, and pelicans, all of which helped turn what could have been an average skyscraper into a modern wonder.

Nearly 7,500 tons of terra cotta were used to achieve the Gothic effect of the Woolworth Building. Other materials used included 17 million bricks, 28,000 tons of tile, 53,000 pounds of bronze and iron hardware, 24,000 tons of steel, and 87 miles of electrical wiring.

BEASTS OF THE AIR AND LAND

Erected in 1915, Rosenwald Hall was part of the second wave of construction of Gothic buildings at the University of Chicago. Holabird and Roche were its architects. The building's many and varied carvings reflect its original mission, for Rosenwald Hall initially housed the departments of geology and geography. Thomas Chrowder Chamberlin, head of the geology department, and Rollin D. Salisbury, head of the geography department, chose subjects for the gargoyles symbolic of their respective disciplines.

ALLIGATORS

Alligators of all shapes, sizes, and demeanors bedeck the exterior of Rosenwald Hall. Shown here are two of the more noteworthy ones.

BIRDS

A duck, eagle, albatross, and condor represent the birds of the air. Pictured here is a duck found on the tower of the University of Chicago's Rosenwald Hall.

CONTINENTAL BEASTS

BUFFALO BILL AND BULLY EUROPE

Found atop the tower of Rosenwald Hall are symbols for the four continents. A buffalo represents North America, while a bull is the standard bearer for Europe. The symbols for Asia and Africa are an elephant and lion, respectively. Shown here are the buffalo and the bull.

TEASING TIGER

Princeton University is noted not only for its fine academics but for the competitive spirit of its athletic teams. The university gymnasium was designed by Aymar Embury II in 1903, to ensure that Princeton students could develop both sound minds and sound bodies. It was partially destroyed by fire in 1944. Rebuilt through the generosity of an alumnus in 1947, it is now known as Dillon Gymnasium. Several outstanding gargoyles were added in the rebuilding.

A tiger prominently positioned at the main entrance of Dillon Gymnasium is the university mascot. With a teasing demeanor, the tiger appears ready to pounce on the next lowly student who crosses the threshold below. Another reason this tiger may look so pleased is that it was ultimately chosen to replace the lion that had been the university's original symbol. The change occurred slowly over the years as the students' preference for the tiger over the lion was acknowledged; the tiger was officially adopted as the symbol in 1911.

MENACING DRAGONS

Donated by Martin A. Ryerson, the second president of the University of Chicago's Board of Trustees, Ryerson Hall is a virtual zoo of gurgling gargoyles and grotesques. Designed by Henry Ives Cobb in 1894, the building represents the best of Gothic on campus and inspired then university president William Rainey Harper to proclaim it "the most beautiful university building in the world."

EAGLE

Eagles are portrayed in many shapes and sizes on the University of Chicago campus. This vicious-looking critter is found on a lavishly decorated Gothic structure built for the study of anatomy, which is still carried on within its walls.

LIVING CREATURES

Constructed in 1909, Guyot Hall is a massive structure on the Princeton University campus. The architectural firm of Parrish and Schroeder designed the building to house the school's biology and geology departments, and its exterior ornamentation reflects the two disciplines. Some of the carvings are believed to be the creations of Gutzon Borglum, who apprenticed at the Cathedral of St. John the Divine in New York City and went on to win national acclaim for his carvings of the presidential heads of Mount Rushmore in South Dakota.

The east end of Guyot Hall houses the biology department and is lavishly decorated with sculptures of living species from the air, land, and sea. Shown here from top left to right are a contemplative ape, bellowing elephant, beastly boar, grim rhinoceros, watched bird, upside-down frog, and ready-to-be-boiled crab.

EXTINCT SPECIES

The geology and geophysics department is located in the west end of the structure, which is appropriately festooned with extinct creatures. Some of its gone-but-not-forgotten species are two types of dinosaurs, a smattering of prehistoric reptilian creatures and precursors to birds as we know them, and a trilobite fossil to remind us of our ultimate fate.

91

4

HUMOR
ON HIGH

"IT WAS LIKE SHAZAAM. I WAS back in the twelfth century," recounts carver Malcolm S. Harlow Jr. of his experience one day high in the air at the Washington National Cathedral. "There I was working with the same tools carvers have used for centuries. I was doing the same work, in the same way, in a similar setting. On that day on the top of that scaffolding, I finally got it. We are part of all that has gone on before." ✳ Even the way carving is taught has remained unchanged over the centuries. It is a trade

93

passed from one generation to the next. "Many of us learned the craft at home, over dinner. Our fathers, our uncles would discuss what went on in the shop that day. We would listen and learn," says Vincenzo Palumbo, a fifth-generation stone carver, who for years worked alongside his father at Washington National Cathedral. Palumbo is now the cathedral's master carver. He explains that experienced carvers can judge the quality of another's work simply by listening. The sound made when a chisel hits stone is enough for trained ears to know when a mistake has been made and also to recognize when a carving will be a masterpiece.

The most significant change over the years in this creative process is that, thanks to cranes, it is a great deal easier to raise blocks of stone high into the sky. Other than that, carvers use the same tools—hammer and chisel—and work under conditions very similar to those of past centuries, although the recent introduction of a pneumatic chisel has created an opportunity for them to work more efficiently and learn new techniques.

MAGICAL MEDUSA AND FRIENDS (PREVIOUS PAGE)

Literally hundreds of sculptures adorn the exterior of Washington National Cathedral. Here on the southwest tower, a menagerie of carvings on nearly every corner joins the gargoyle Medusa at her spot 578 feet above ground. A mix of all of God's creatures—pigs, elephants, and even angels—reflects the diversity of the nation for which this church was built.

Like the carving, good gargoyle design remains largely unchanged. It requires both an interesting silhouette or outline so the design can be discerned from afar and contrasts in textures to give the gargoyle better feature definition and composition. Because gargoyles are viewed from the bottom up, more attention and detailing must be given to the underside of the sculpture than to the top, which makes it necessary for designers to rearrange their creative process. "We have to visualize things not from what they will look like directly head-on, but what they might look like from, say, five hundred feet above someone's head. It is a different way of visualizing, thinking, and creating," explains sculptor Jay Hall Carpenter, who was trained by master carvers at Washington National Cathedral.

One of the challenges posed by this creative process is producing the right amount of exaggeration in a carving. To make an object visible from below, features, details, and symbols have to be magnified somewhat in order to make a statement, portray a symbol, poke fun at something, or simply convey a feeling. It takes skill, training, imagination, and a bit of luck to get it right.

What has changed in the creative process is the subject matter of many carvings. Today, American gargoyles and their counterparts may be terrifying in appearance, but they can also be irreverent, gentle, humorous, or socially conscious, depending upon the inspiration of their creators. Like their older European counterparts, however, they continue to tell a story, relay a message, and pique the curiosity and imagination of viewers.

THE CROOKED POLITICIAN

Contrary to rumors that float around Washington National Cathedral from time to time, the crooked politician gargoyle was not modeled after anyone in particular. Sculptor Jay Hall Carpenter wanted to mock some of the more outrageous elements of the Washington power structure. He jokingly explains that the crooked politician simply evolved from "the hole in its head."

Some of the characteristics of crooked politicians are readily visible. The horns sticking out from the gargoyle's head signal an affiliation with the devil. The robust belly alludes to regular participation in the reception circuit. And the cigar signifies deals being made behind closed doors in smoke-filled rooms. Other symbols are less obvious. A wad of hundred-dollar bills pokes out of the carving's left coat pocket, while on the right, the scales of justice are being tampered with.

Carver Walter Arnold mounted Carpenter's half-scale clay model next to its designated stone block on the building. And in 1981, like his counterparts from centuries past, Arnold worked on the piece from his perch high in the air, oblivious to the crowds who watched him from below.

ELEPHANT WITH BOOK

The primary donor for this gargoyle on Washington National Cathedral is a former manager of the Cathedral's bookstore. Sculptor Frederick E. Hart designed it to reflect both the donor's love of books and the balancing act required to run a successful bookstore. An elephant was chosen because of its fabled ability to remember everything—a prime requirement for making a successful go of it in the book world. Malcolm S. Harlow Jr. carved the extraordinary image in 1975.

MEDUSA

Legend has it that Medusa was a pretty maiden who took great pride in her beautiful hair. Her charms aroused the jealousy of Minerva and the goddess used her powers to turn Medusa's lovely locks into hissing serpents, leaving the girl so hideous that anyone who caught sight of her turned to stone.

This modern-day Medusa on Washington National Cathedral was intended as a pun. Rather than turning those who look at her into stone, Medusa herself has been cast forever in stone. Reflecting her vanity, she holds a cracked mirror in her hand. Wriggling wildly, the snakes in her hair seem to be trying to escape from the stone. Jay Hall Carpenter designed Medusa, one of the eight largest gargoyles on the cathedral. Wayne D. Ferree carved the intricate piece, which was installed in 1987.

MISSOURI BEAR

Wanting its state to be permanently represented on the building, the Eastern Missouri Committee of the National Cathedral Association donated this gargoyle in the early 1970s. Sculptor Donald R. Miller intertwined several symbols of the grand state of Missouri into one gargoyle. The bear itself represents the two standing bears on the Missouri state seal, with its motto, "We can stand on our own." The animal is shown peering through the famous "Gateway to the West" arch of St. Louis. It was carved by Constantine Seferlis, who was renowned for his ability to incorporate accurate anatomical features into whimsical designs.

THIEF

A greedy thief is caught in the act in this gargoyle on Washington National Cathedral. Wearing a business suit, a longhaired man holds a pig under his left arm and a rooster in his right hand, while a dog tugs at his sleeve. Sculptor Constantine Seferlis wanted to show not only the consequences of excessive greed but also the power of small forces to affect outcomes. The irony of the carving is that this thief has been caught not by the police or even by a higher power; rather, it is a small dog that impedes his escape. Seferlis also carved the piece, which was placed on the cathedral in 1975.

ARMY MULE

An army mule with bared teeth and ears on alert was donated by the wife of a U.S. Army colonel in his memory. Placed on Washington National Cathedral in 1979, it is another example of the collaboration between sculptor Carl L. Bush and carver Frederick E. Hart.

SEA HORSE

One of thirteen gargoyles on First Presbyterian Church in Pittsburgh, this sea-horse-like creature seems a bit out of place, given that the church is located in a sea of concrete. One exception to the urban surroundings is the historic graveyard that separates First Presbyterian Church from the adjacent Trinity Cathedral, providing a tranquil green spot from which to view this charming piece.

CANDID CAMERAMAN

This gargoyle on Washington National Cathedral is a study of the unexpected. Sculptor Rubin Peacock designed a duck wearing a necktie decorated with the ace of hearts and clothing festooned with diamonds and spades. When one looks more closely, however, the whimsical gargoyle holds a secret in its mouth: the scrunched-up face of a photographer is seen peering from behind a camera!

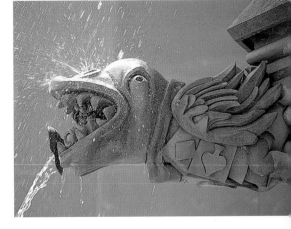

Explains Malcolm S. Harlow Jr., who carved the piece in the early 1970s, "I thought it would be fun to poke a little fun at the tourists." Having worked in situ high above the gawking tourists, Harlow had a real sense of what it was like to "look down from above." This humorous carving is his payback for all the pictures taken of him while he was closer to the heavens than to the earth.

LAUGHTER GENERATORS

Found on buildings across America are gargoyles whose sole mission appears to be to invite laughter. These laugh-along creatures, with their silly demeanors, absurd postures, and infectious smiles, capture the imagination of the amused viewer.

SQUARE-JAW ALLIGATOR

Visitors to Washington National Cathedral can't help but chuckle when they catch a glimpse of this smiling gator designed by Carl M. Tucker. Tucker spent more than a decade at the cathedral as an artisan, where he was known as a Renaissance man for his vast knowledge and musical talent. He came up with the idea for this happy-looking creature and presented it to Richard T. Feller, then clerk of the works, who ordered it carved. Tucker's one and only gargoyle to appear on the cathedral was carved by Edward Ratti.

BELLYACHE

Suffering from overindulgence? This beast has feathered arms and little hands that are clutching a bulging belly. Its sculptor, Juliet Fazan, was one of the winners of the Washington National Cathedral's 1959–60 Gargoyle Design Contest. Then a young Englishwoman doing graduate work at Mount Holyoke, she went on to become a professor of English at the University of Alberta. The carver of the piece, which was installed in 1964, is not known.

TOOTHACHE NO MORE

A dragonlike beast clutches a molar as he clings to Washington National Cathedral for dear life by only a thumb. Constantine Seferlis designed and carved this piece in 1976 knowing that it would draw laughter from visitors. Absurd or not, the sculpture also stands as a fitting tribute to its honoree, a physicist at the National Bureau of Standards, who researched materials for the replacement of teeth.

CONVERSATION

The gentle, intimate conversation depicted here demonstrates the shift from hideous and frightening gargoyles to more humorous and humanistic creatures. This carving, located in the central portal of the western facade of the Cathedral of St. John the Divine in upper Manhattan, is part of an intricately carved facade that blends new and old, serious and humorous, beautiful and ugly. It stands out among many because of both its subject matter and the use of color in the sculptures behind it.

The two stone creatures are also unique because they show the evolution of the cathedral as work progressed. John Angel carved the attentive anteater-like creature on the left in the 1940s. Simon Verity, who has served as the cathedral's master carver since 1988, completed the dog on the right in 1996.

Verity took carving at the cathedral back to its roots. He worked directly on stone from drawings rather than models. He even went so far as to introduce color into his carvings, as had his medieval brethren. Explains Verity, "I needed color in my life. I spent ten years of my life carving these things and I needed something other than monochrome." Verity painted his carving using a colored pigment made from ground stone that was mixed in casein, a milk-based glue. The yellow, purple, and red tones come from iron deposits in the stone, while the green shades come from copper. True to form, these are colors that would have been available during the medieval period.

MONKEY CLOWNS

In 1896, Francis Landey Patton, president of what was then known as the College of New Jersey, announced that the institution was changing its name to Princeton University. With the name change, Patton predicted that Princeton would become an internationally known university of the caliber of Oxford and Cambridge. Of course, the easiest way to become like these prestigious universities was to look like them. Thus, for the next fifty years, every building on campus was designed in a collegiate Gothic style, emulating the fine learning establishments across the Atlantic. Patton Hall, in fact, looks like a medieval castle, complete with parapets, turrets, and gargoyles. Along the turrets, monkeys dressed as clowns mock those who dare to look up rather than keep their eyes fixed ahead of them.

According to Hugh de N. Wynne, a highly knowledgeable 1939 Princeton graduate, monkeys were frequently chosen as subjects for two reasons. First, they are rambunctious creatures, as are students. Second, monkeys are considered a lower life-form to humans, much as students are to professors. The monkey depicted at left is yelling at the top of his lungs and, not surprisingly, not being heard. The second monkey thumbs his nose and sticks out his tongue at visitors.

MONKEY MAGIC

President Woodrow Wilson graduated with the Princeton class of 1879 and later became president of the university. His office was located in 1879 Hall, which was built by the class of '79 on the occasion of its twenty-fifth reunion. Designed by Benjamin Wistar Morris Jr., 1879 Hall boasts a number of monkeys, many of which are engaged in activities beyond their comprehension.

ROAD RAGE

Here another Princeton monkey demonstrates his lack of brain matter. Depicted with driver's glasses, his hat covering a wild hairdo to match a crazed look, the beast seems perplexed by the car's steering wheel. If he was ever to figure it out, one could imagine that his driving experience might end in road rage.

MONKEY WITH A CAMERA

Perched on the west side of 1879 Hall, this candid cameraman is fascinated by a toy he doesn't know is a tool, which is how many lifelong endeavors and careers begin. Gutzon Borglum, sculptor extraordinaire, is said to have created this crazy ape.

CONFUSED HORSE

On a turret of Patton Hall on Princeton University's campus is a horse that has lost his way. The riderless horse is saddled, ready to go, but appears confused despite his monocle. Symbolic of the predicament of many students, he appears to be searching for someone to tell him what to do, where to go, and how to get there.

COMPETITORS

Two rams lock horns in fierce battle on Bartlett Gymnasium at the University of Chicago, imagery that appropriately depicts the many competitive events that take place within the lavishly decorated building. With parapets, arched doorways, and carvings of scenes from Sir Walter Scott's *Ivanhoe,* the gymnasium, constructed in 1904, was designed by the architectural firm of Sheply, Rutan and Coolidge. During World War II, Bartlett Gymnasium served a military function befitting its fortresslike design when it was used as a barracks for the U.S. Navy.

CROWNED DOG

The crowned dog that appears above a fourth-floor window of Tribune Tower in Chicago is shown with his paw in a mousetrap, paying a price for his pomposity. Architects John Mead Howells and Raymond M. Hood designed Tribune Tower and obviously had some fun in the process when they added grotesques to the exterior. Little is known, however, about the carvers who actually created these sculptures. Explains sculptor Walter Arnold, who restored a number of the grotesques during a recent renovation of the building, "Builders would not have thought to keep track of who carved what any more than they would have thought to keep track of which carpenter or cabinetmaker did a piece of work for them."

ALERT FROG

On the exterior of Chicago's Tribune Tower, a massive Gothic building signifying the power and prestige of the press, this small frog is said to represent those who are ever alert and eager to be heard.

SCANDALIZED ELEPHANT

What could be a clearer depiction of scandal than a big stinky elephant forever holding its nose? Carved from Indiana limestone from Hoadley's Quarry, which is still in operation today in Bloomington, Indiana, this scandalous elephant on Tribune Tower provokes both laughter and thoughtfulness from those who take a moment to consider what it represents.

5

IN MAN'S IMAGE

DELIVERING A SPIRITUAL MESSAGE was the raison d'être for early European gargoyles. In contrast, most modern American gargoyles deliver messages that are clearly secular and rooted in the materialistic society in which we live. This transformation reflects the evolution from spiritual to secular that has taken place throughout Western art and helps to explain the continuing power of gargoyles to fascinate and inspire contemporary viewers. Many gargoyles are decidedly modern images

that depict the culture, values, and issues of our times—most often with a sense of humor. Sculptors at Washington National Cathedral were, in fact, discouraged from researching historical gargoyles so that their designs would be fresh, current, and appropriate to the times in which they were carved. As a result, gargoyle subjects there have evolved from mythical creatures to animals to humans—a shift that has been replicated on building exteriors all across America.

Modern carvings are a reflection of everyday life. Jay Hall Carpenter gets most of his ideas while driving. Malcolm S. Harlow Jr. is inspired by the people he knows. He has incorporated into his carv-

PIPES OF PAN (PREVIOUS PAGE)

Frederick E. Hart sculpted this piece in 1975, which depicts Pan, a satyr with pointed ears, tiny horns, human hands, furry legs, and cloven hooves. The craftsmen who worked on it jokingly referred to the carving as the "Pipes of Pan," which, as it turned out, was an appropriate reference: the gargoyle was donated in thanksgiving for the musical programs of Washington National Cathedral.

Carver Malcolm S. Harlow Jr. somewhat altered the original design to accommodate an exceedingly large mouth and stuck the creature's thumbnail into its jugular vein to give him a reason for perpetually screaming.

ings the features of his coworkers, a flower design he saw in a dress, and a colleague's gestures. For Constantine Seferlis, inspiration comes from his teachers in Greece, who taught traditional methods of drawing and sculpting. These he uses to create sculptures of timely topics that reveal his exceptional ability to capture anatomy. "Its perfection," he says, "could turn an atheist into a believer."

Although many of the sculptors and carvers whose magnificent creations fill these pages now lie dead and buried, their essence remains alive in their work. Their artistry is still visible. Their messages still have meaning. Their humor still sparks laughter.

To ensure the continuation of this art form, a number of present-day sculptors and carvers are working to instruct a new generation of men and women in how to turn a piece of stone into a piece of art. Walter Arnold, for one, consistently brings in young apprentices to work side by side with him in his studio in Park Ridge, Illinois. He believes it is his obligation to pass on the lessons he learned when he was sixteen and traveled to Italy to learn from the masters there. Constantine Seferlis also continues to work every day in a studio in the backyard of his home outside of Washington, D.C. There, among the trees and the squirrels, he gently guides the young apprentices who do the hard physical labor of making his designs come to life in stone.

FLASHING CAVEMAN

The last gargoyle to be placed on Washington National Cathedral is the Flashing Caveman. This gargoyle also completed a creative cycle for sculptor Jay Hall Carpenter since it was the last of eight he designed as a series. Carpenter designed his first gargoyle, a hara-kiri-committing gremlin with a knife stuck in its belly, when he was seventeen. In 1977, at the age of twenty-five, he designed the last gargoyle, one that depicts the result of the knife's work. Here, the caveman's belly is cut wide open, his entrails visible for all to see. Because of the position of the hands, it appears as though the gargoyle is "flashing" his organs. The rest of the caveman's appearance is what one might expect for a raging madman. Caught openmouthed in a wail, he has wild hair and an unkempt beard.

119

THE GRANDSONS

This pair of gargoyles on Washington National Cathedral depicts two different types of behavior. The first gargoyle is of a young boy with his arms around his knees and a wagon at his feet. Reflecting his good behavior, there is a halo around his head. The second gargoyle is not as well behaved as the first. He sits with a cookie jar between his feet, a stolen cookie in his left hand. Not surprisingly, his halo is broken.

The donors of these gargoyles gave them in thanksgiving for their two young grandsons. Reportedly, the boys' grandmother never confided in them which gargoyle represented which grandson. It was her desire to keep the boys guessing as a way to inspire good behavior in each. The boys, now grown men, are still guessing. Carl L. Bush sculpted both gargoyles in 1970. Vincenzo Palumbo carved the "good grandson" and Constantine Seferlis carved the "not-so-good" grandson.

CURLY LOCKS WITH LYRE

Curly Locks with Lyre was given in tribute to the work of Andrew Tietjen, who served as organist and choir conductor at the Washington National Cathedral for many years. This menacing musical beast, opposite, was a gift from a family of longtime musical contributors to Washington National Cathedral: Tietjen's daughter is a member of the Cathedral Choral Society and her two sons sang in the cathedral's choir. Malcolm S. Harlow Jr. sculpted and carved the piece in 1975.

THE BUSINESSMAN

Sculptor and carver Constantine Seferlis was given a free hand in designing a gargoyle for Washington National Cathedral in honor of a successful New York corporate executive. The only restriction imposed was that he had to incorporate the honoree's rather large nose into the design. The result is a wonderfully fun gargoyle, dubbed the "Yuppie," who is depicted in his rush to get to work on Monday morning. The carving is hung from a limb to signify risk taking. Seferlis added a briefcase, dollar sign, and divining rod to complete the caricature of a man on the move, ready to tackle the world. The Businessman was reportedly a surprise gift from the wife and friends of the man portrayed, who is said to have been delighted with the finished sculpture installed in 1976.

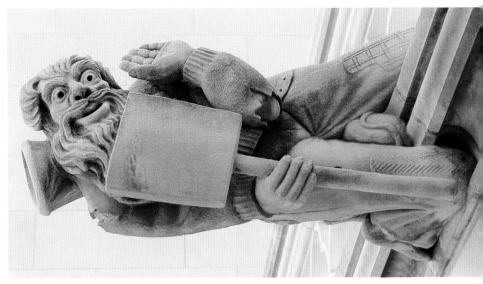

THE HIPPIE

Located a mere three feet from a window on the turret stairs of one of Washington National Cathedral's west towers, this is a carving that people can see quite easily and can actually touch. Given its uniquely accessible location, then-clerk of the works Richard T. Feller instructed sculptor Constantine Seferlis to design something that represented the times. Seferlis did as instructed and carved a gentle, humorous symbol for all those who came of age during the 1970s.

The hippie gargoyle captures a great deal of the times—from his placard representing the many protests of the era to a loaf of bread indicating its easy communal living. Upon closer examination, viewers can see that the hippie, eschewing materialism, has patches on his trousers and holes in his old sweater. The figure is prepared for anything: Seferlis added a bag of marijuana between its legs!

The technical novelty of this gargoyle is that it isn't a true gargoyle at all. Although designed to give the impression that water would spout from the bell of a toy horn rather than through the more traditional mouth opening, the lead pipe for drainage was never installed. Thus, it is a nonfunctioning but nonetheless very appealing gargoyle.

ADMINISTRATOR

Artist Peter Rockwell, son of renowned illustrator Norman Rockwell, and carver Malcolm S. Harlow Jr. created this gargoyle in 1975, which depicts a harried-looking administrator. Located on Washington National Cathedral, the carving of a balding man with huge ears, tiny legs, and big shoes appears to be nearly jumping off the building to make a point. The donor of this gargoyle served as past president of the National Cathedral Association and overseer of the cathedral's capital campaign for ten years.

MASTER CARVER

Most people who knew him agree that Washington National Cathedral master carver Roger Morigi was a perfectionist and had a temper to match. This gargoyle, titled Master Carver, was designed and carved in secret by John Guarente. When it was unveiled, Morigi reportedly nearly blew his top. Later he came to recognize it as a personal tribute to his work and always took visitors to see his likeness on the building that he had helped to shape.

The expert carver is half man and half devil, with horns, a forked tail, and one cloven hoof. An atomic mushroom cloud rising from his head evokes Morigi's legendary temper. He was an avid golfer and so his gargoyle is attired in a short-sleeve golf shirt. The figure holds a chisel in his left hand, a mallet in his right, and peeking out of his left pant pocket are sculptors' tools. In his right pocket, one can see a pistol, a dagger, and a flask, tongue-in-cheek references to Morigi's Italian heritage.

BOY WITH BICEPS

A universal image of the benefits of exercise graces the parapet of the University of Chicago's Bartlett Gymnasium. Given the mischievous expression on the carving's face, one can only wonder if his biceps are real or imagined. Donated by trustee Adolphus C. Bartlett, the elaborate exterior decoration of the gymnasium celebrates the life of the son of the donor, Frank Dickinson Bartlett, who died at the age of twenty.

BUGEYES

Designed by Peter Rockwell, who carries the creative genes of his father, Norman Rockwell, and carved by master carver Vincenzo Palumbo, this naked figure with long flowing hair represents intergenerational talent. Peter Rockwell is an artist in his own right, as is Vincenzo Palumbo, who worked alongside his father, Paul Palumbo, at Washington National Cathedral for many years.

Of note, this is one of the few gargoyles carved by Vincenzo Palumbo. Although he's been a carver at Washington National Cathedral for nearly forty years, he preferred to work on larger, more intricate ornamental pieces. However, when he took up a subject, the result was grand, as is evidenced by this piece, which was placed on the cathedral in 1977.

GENTLE BOY

Tucked away on Washington National Cathedral is a gargoyle of a young boy holding a fish, with a book and puppy at his feet, which was donated by parents in honor of their son. Artist William Conrad Severson captured the gentle relationship between a boy and his dog, and the piece was artfully carved by Malcolm S. Harlow Jr. in 1977.

BISHOP

One hopes that this bishop with his mouth wide open is spewing out the Word of God for the edification of all who pass below. Attired like a man of the cloth, the gargoyle on Washington National Cathedral wears a stole and holds a crosier in one hand and the end of his cincture in the other. Carved by Vincenzo Palumbo in 1976, the gargoyle was designed by Constantine Seferlis in memory of Robert Tate Allan, an editor and the publisher of a religious newsletter, who was known to his friends as "Bishop."

FOOTBALL RUNNER

Designed by R. C. Gildersleeve, McCosh Hall on the Princeton University campus is literally bedecked with grotesques along its exterior. One of its more notorious examples, the Football Runner, is pictured here. The halfback is running at full speed, head held high, ball under arm, toward an invisible goal line. The player is attired in the football apparel of the early 1900s as McCosh Hall was built in 1907.

BARBELL BOY

Even in the early 1900s, working out didn't always work out. Here, a chubby fellow is depicted struggling to lift his weights, although the oversize weights have clearly overwhelmed the lifter. Barbell Boy can be found on Dillon Gymnasium at Princeton University.

MAN AND BEAST

Four large gargoyles were added to the facade of Dillon Gymnasium at Princeton University in 1947. One of them depicts an ape, which campus lore describes as lecturing on Darwin. Another is of a professor engrossed in a book that contains only four pages. The learned professor bears striking similarities to the literate ape. Both hold open books, wear half-glasses, sport a goatee, and appear earnest. The resemblance is explained in the campus gargoyle tour with the rhyme:

> *Said the ape as it swung by its tail,*
> *To its children both female and male,*
> *"From your children, my dears,*
> *In a couple of years,*
> *May evolve a professor at Yale."*

HULL GATE

Despite the desire of its benefactor, John D. Rockefeller, to free the University of Chicago from financial constraints, the reality is that money did matter in its design and construction. When the board of trustees offered the campus architect Henry Ives Cobb a budget of $50,000 to design a gate in honor of his contributions to the university, Cobb declined. Campus legend has it that Cobb found the offer insultingly meager and instead designed and donated a gate to the university so he could maintain control over it.

Although the grotesques that line either side of this structure are not technically gargoyles, they are included here because they are among the most celebrated carvings on campus. For generations of students, they have depicted the climb up the educational ladder at this renowned institution of higher learning.

THE DRAGONS

Cobb's sense of humor is evident in the carvings of two dragons on either side of the gate that represent impediments to gaining admittance to the university. The dragon on the left is said to represent the financial aid officer; the dragon on the right is the admissions officer.

THE SENIOR

"Ah, how sweet it is!" The proud senior stands at the top of the slippery slope and sticks out its tongue at the lower life-forms below.

THE JUNIOR

The smug figure representing the third-year class snarls at the figure below it, keeping the lower classmen in their place, while straining to reach the top.

THE SOPHOMORE

This bug-eyed figure symbolizes second-year students. After surviving the freshman's trial by fire, the creature appears more confident as it looks upward.

THE FRESHMAN

The University of Chicago is one of the few remaining universities in the nation that divides the academic year into quarters rather than semesters; this means the workload is heavy and the time to complete it short. The difficult adjustment that must be made by each incoming class is depicted in this carving with its tenuous grip and unsure footing.

DUELING QUALITIES

Intricate grotesques along the fourth floor and the top balcony at the twenty-fifth floor help to humanize Tribune Tower by offering social commentary on the trials and tribulations of modern life. The carvings were often grouped in twos to depict opposite qualities of the human experience. A sample of these social groupings include the following:

RADICALISM AND CONSERVATISM

The wild and vicious wolf represents radicalism and stands in contrast to conservatism, exemplified in its companion, a passive dog.

ACTIVITY AND INDOLENCE

The ape and bear represent opposite characteristics or virtues, depending upon the viewpoint of the observer. Here the ape portrays activity and the bear represents indolence.

CITIZEN AND ANARCHIST

Peacefully contemplating a book, a sheep represents positive, responsible public behavior. This law-abiding behavior is juxtaposed with that of a gorilla clutching a dagger, which represents anarchy.

NEWS AND RUMOR

Above the main entrance of Tribune Tower is the flaming head of a shouting man, who represents news. Hot or not, the grotesque apparently wants its news to be heard. Insidious Rumor is depicted to the left of News. Here, a winged man is shown with his fingers to his lips, supposedly telling a story, but not necessarily one based on fact. Look closely to see the dagger stuck in his forehead, a reminder, perhaps, of the consequences of spreading rumors.

IN MEMORIAM

Sitting on scaffolding hundreds of feet off the ground to carve a gargoyle in situ can be uncomfortable work at best, dangerous at worst. Joseph Ratti was one of the unlucky few who gave his life to his craft in 1955, while preparing to carve a gargoyle on Washington National Cathedral. These blocks remain uncarved in his memory. This image is shared here to honor him and his colleagues everywhere who put their lives at risk to create magical creatures from stone.

RESOURCES

Washington National Cathedral
Gift Shop
202-537-6200

ADDITIONAL
INFORMATION

Allegheny Historic Preservation
Society, Inc.
971 Beech Avenue
Pittsburgh, PA 15233
412-323-1070
412-231-4440 (fax)

Chicago Architecture Foundation
224 South Michigan Avenue
Chicago, IL 60604-2507
312-922-3432
312-922-0481 (fax)

Friends of Terra Cotta, Inc.
c/o Tunick
771 West End Avenue 10E
New York, NY 10025
212-662-0768

Historical Society of Western
Pennsylvania
Library and Archives
1212 Smallman Street
Pittsburgh, PA 15222
412-454-6000
www.pghhistory.org

Pittsburgh History & Landmarks
Foundation
One Station Square, Suite 450
Pittsburgh, PA 15219-1170
412-471-5808
412-471-1633 (fax)

The Skyscraper Museum
110 Maiden Lane
New York, NY 10005
212-968-1961
www.skyscraper.org

GARGOYLE PRODUCTS

California Gargoyles
Lighthouse International
P.O. Box 15084
Scottsdale, AZ 85267-5084
480-391-9747
www.webcom.com/gargoyle/order.
html

Design Toscano
1635 Greenleaf Avenue
Elk Grove, IL 60007-5526
800-525-0733

NOVUS Enterprises
401 East Campbell Avenue
Campbell, CA 95008
888-NOVUS-90
408-374-5210
408-374-5203 (fax)
smith000@ix.netcom.com

WEB SITES

www.aardvarkelectric.com/
gargoyle
www.aaweb.com/fred/store/
perlshop.egi
www.elore.com/elfs405
www.ils.unc.edu/gargoyle/nathist
www.library.wustl.edu/~spec/
archives/gargoyle
www.masteryinc.com/gargoyle/
owners
www.oasispro.com/keepers
www.stonecarver.com
www.webcom.com/gargoyle/
catalog

RECOMMENDED READING

Bruce, H. Addington. *Above the Clouds and Old New York*. New York: The Woolworth Company, 1913.

Cochran, Edward A. *The Cathedral of Commerce*. New York: Thomsen-Ellis Company, 1927.

DeBienville, Michael. *Gargoyles*. New York: Andrews McMeel Publishing, 1996.

Feller, Richard T. *Completing Washington National Cathedral for Thy Great Glory*. Washington, D.C.: Washington National Cathedral, 1989.

Foote, Ray A. *The David J. Mahoney Photographic Collection of Gargoyles on the Quadrangle at the University of Pennsylvania*, 1986. Available in the University of Pennsylvania Archives.

Gorman, James F., Jeffrey A. Cohen, George E. Thomas, G. Holmes Perkins. *Drawing Toward Building: Philadelphia Architectural Graphics 1732–1986*. Philadelphia: University of Pennsylvania Press, 1986.

Hunt, Marjorie. *The Stone Carvers: Master Craftsmen of Washington National Cathedral*. Washington, D.C.: Smithsonian Institution Press, 1999.

Kamin, Blair. *Tribune Tower: American Landmark, Commentary by Blair Kamin*. Chicago: Tribune Company, 2000.

Nichols, John P. *Skyline Queen and the Merchant Prince: The Woolworth Story*. New York: Pocket Books, 1973.

Quirk, Howard E. *The Living Cathedral: St. John the Divine*. New York: The Crossroad Publishing Company, 1993.

Rebold Benton, Janetta. *Holy Terrors: Gargoyles on Medieval Buildings*. New York: Abbeville Press, 1997.

Shaff, Howard, and Audrey Karl Shaff. *Six Wars at a Time: The Life and Times of Gutzon Borglum*. Sioux Falls, S.D.: Center for Western Studies at Augustana College, 1985.

Tigerman, Stanley. *Chicago Tribune Tower Competition*. New York: Rizzoli International Publications, 1980.

Tribune Company. *Tribune Tower*. Chicago: The Tribune Company, 1968.

Tunick, Susan. *Terra-Cotta Skyline*. New York: Princeton Architectural Press, 1997.

University of Chicago. *A Walking Guide to the Campus*. Chicago: The University of Chicago, 1991.

Van Trump, James D. *Life and Architecture in Pittsburgh*. Pittsburgh: Pittsburgh History & Landmarks Foundation, 1983.

———. *The Gothic Revived in Pittsburgh: A Medievalistic Excursion*. Pittsburgh: Pittsburgh History and Landmarks Foundation.

Washington National Cathedral. *Washington National Cathedral*. Washington, D.C.: Washington National Cathedral, 1995.

Winkler, John K. *Five and Ten: The Fabulous Life of F. W. Woolworth*. New York: Robert M. McBride & Company, 1940.

ACKNOWLEDGMENTS

I could not have written this book without the help of many wonderful people. Some lent their knowledge to me. Others interrupted their lives to make sure I found the information I needed. Still others fed me, housed me, gave me directions, and made me laugh. In my view, *American Gargoyles* is a collective effort that could not have been accomplished without each and every person who appears below.

The staff at Washington National Cathedral devoted a great deal of time, energy, and spirit to help this book come to fruition. My heartfelt thanks to the following individuals: Dr. Charles S. Tidball, Andy Seferlis, and Margie Ward, the cathedral's resident gargoyle experts, who answered my queries on more occasions than I care to count; Canon Richard T. Feller, who shared his historical perspective of the cathedral with me; archivist Dr. Richard Hewlett, who dug through dusty boxes for me; product development manager Erik

Vochinsky, who helped secure the necessary permission to proceed, then lent his editorial guidance to the project; and masons foreman Joe Alonso, who took me on a tour of the cathedral to high places where few have the opportunity to see.

Special thanks is due the creators of the gargoyles. These talented and generous artisans include Jay Hall Carpenter, Malcolm S. Harlow Jr., Constantine Seferlis, Walter Arnold, and Vincenzo Palumbo.

Others who gave considerably of their time and knowledge include Hugh de N. Wynne and Laurel Masten Cantor, who collectively know more about the carvings at Princeton University than any ten experts combined. The folks at the Cathedral of St. John the Divine graciously shared their expertise and interest in the carvings. They are Wayne Kempton, archivist for the Episcopal Diocese of New York; Andrea Yost, education coordinator extraordinaire; Herb

Katz, director of PR; Steve Facey, executive vice-president; and sculptors Simon Verity and Jean-Claude Marchionni, who continue to add to the rich detail of the world's longest cathedral. Robin Borglum Carter also helped considerably with information on her grandfather Gutzon Borglum.

Thanks to Mark Landstrom, Gail Fenske, and Susan Tunick for helping me pull together the story behind the Woolworth Building; Marty Hackett for his assistance at the University of Pennsylvania; and archivist Michael Lampen for the story behind the wyverns of Grace Cathedral. In Pittsburgh, there are many to thank. Those who shared their knowledge about the griffins at the top of Calvary United Methodist Church were the Reverend Tom Funk; professor of history and decorative arts Alice Greller; and Anthony Wolfe, the grandson of one of the architects. Shirley Starrett, church historian at the First Presbyterian Church, provided invaluable assistance. And special thanks to Mary Ann Eubanks of the Pittsburgh History & Landmarks Foundation, who took me on a three-hour walking tour of that fine city to convince me that it had to be included in the project!

A number of Chicagoans also deserve my gratitude for their willingness to share stories, pictures, and time—according to my scheduling needs. Much thanks to Blair Kamin, architecture critic for the *Chicago Tribune*; Faith Brown, director of corporate communications; and Al Gramzinski, general manager of Tribune Tower. The University of Chicago could not have been written without the expertise of gargoyle expert Professor Michael Camille; landscape architect Richard Bumstead; Larry Arbeiter of the news department; and John Biedler, my tour guide, who went above and beyond the call of duty to make sure all of my questions were answered.

And, I couldn't have done it without those who provided food, shelter, and entertainment during my travels. My heartfelt thanks to Rhonda Buckner and Diane Ullius, who took me under their wing, gave me a key to their house, and made me always feel at home when I was away from home. Carl and Nancy Shea also deserve my gratitude, for they cooked me fabulous meals and made certain I never got lost. I had the great fortune of barging in on my old college roommate and dear friend Marian Cosmides, who gave me a place to rest my head but kept me up too late talking to ever get the full benefit of it! And thanks to my family members who live in Pittsburgh and who often accompanied me on my gargoyle treks, with a special thanks to my sister Kathie, who found some irresistible ones there so I could visit more often.

Last but not least, I'd like to thank those who inspired me by sticking in there with me. I am grateful to my husband, Steve Detoy, who supported me literally and figuratively all along the bumpy way to getting published. Special thanks to my daughter Cydnee, who viewed my dream as a reality, and to my elder daughter Marishka, who believed that I could do anything I set my mind to doing.

My friend and lawyer, John Ward, deserves much gratitude for not only coming up with the idea for this book, but then ironing out the details so it could become a reality. I am also grateful to my friend and agent, Julie Hill, whose undying belief in this book, and my ability to write it, helped make it come to life. And finally, I am most grateful for the opportunity to work with my editor, Annetta Hanna, whose clear thinking and attention to detail made my manuscript better each time she took her purple pen in hand.

INDEX